THE HAWK IN THE RAIN

TED HUGHES

*The Hawk in
the Rain*

faber and faber

LONDON · BOSTON

First published in 1957
by Faber and Faber Limited
3 Queen Square London WC1N 3AU
First published in this edition 1968
Reprinted 1970, 1972, 1976, 1979, 1984, 1986 and 1989

Filmset by Wilmaset Birkenhead Wirral
Printed in Great Britain by
Richard Clay Ltd Bungay Suffolk
All rights reserved

ISBN 0 571 08614 4

To Sylvia

ACKNOWLEDGEMENTS

Accent: Billet-Doux; *The Atlantic Monthly:* The Hawk in the Rain; *The BBC Third Programme* and *Poetry* (Chicago): The Martyrdom of Bishop Farrar; *Harper's:* The Dove Breeder; *The London Magazine:* Famous Poet; *The Nation:* The Hag; Roarers in a Ring; Wind; *Poetry* (Chicago): The Casualty; The Jaguar; The Ancient Heroes and the Bomber Pilot.

The Hawk in the Rain was chosen to receive the First Publication Award in a contest conducted by the Poetry Center of the Young Men's and Young Women's Hebrew Association of New York City in co-operation with Harper & Brothers.

CONTENTS

9

The Hawk in the Rain

I drown in the drumming ploughland, I drag up
Heel after heel from the swallowing of the earth's mouth,
From clay that clutches my each step to the ankle
With the habit of the dogged grave, but the hawk

Effortlessly at height hangs his still eye.
His wings hold all creation in a weightless quiet,
Steady as a hallucination in the streaming air.
While banging wind kills these stubborn hedges,

Thumbs my eyes, throws my breath, tackles my heart,
And rain hacks my head to the bone, the hawk hangs
The diamond point of will that polestars
The sea drowner's endurance: and I,

Bloodily grabbed dazed last-moment-counting
Morsel in the earth's mouth, strain towards the master-
Fulcrum of violence where the hawk hangs still.
That maybe in his own time meets the weather

Coming the wrong way, suffers the air, hurled upside down,
Fall from his eye, the ponderous shires crash on him,
The horizon traps him; the round angelic eye
Smashed, mix his heart's blood with the mire of the land.

The Jaguar

The apes yawn and adore their fleas in the sun.
The parrots shriek as if they were on fire, or strut
Like cheap tarts to attract the stroller with the nut.
Fatigue with indolence, tiger and lion

Lie still as the sun. The boa-constrictor's coil
Is a fossil. Cage after cage seems empty, or
Stinks of sleepers from the breathing straw.
It might be painted on a nursery wall.

But who runs like the rest past these arrives
At a cage where the crowd stands, stares, mesmerized,
As a child at a dream, at a jaguar hurrying enraged
Through prison darkness after the drills of his eyes

On a short fierce fuse. Not in boredom –
The eye satisfied to be blind in fire,
By the bang of blood in the brain deaf the ear –
He spins from the bars, but there's no cage to him

More than to the visionary his cell:
His stride is wildernesses of freedom:
The world rolls under the long thrust of his heel.
Over the cage floor the horizons come.

Macaw and Little Miss

In a cage of wire-ribs
The size of a man's head, the macaw bristles in a staring
Combustion, suffers the stoking devils of his eyes.
In the old lady's parlour, where an aspidistra succumbs
To the musk of faded velvet, he hangs as in clear flames,
   Like a torturer's iron instrument preparing
    With dense slow shudderings of greens, yellows, blues,
      Crimsoning into the barbs:

   Or like the smouldering head that hung
In Killdevil's brass kitchen, in irons, who had been
Volcano swearing to vomit the world away in black ash,
And would, one day; or a fugitive aristocrat
From some thunderous mythological hierarchy, caught
   By a little boy with a crust and a bent pin,
    Or snare of horsehair set for a song-thrush,
      And put in a cage to sing.

   The old lady who feeds him seeds
Has a grand-daughter. The girl calls him 'Poor Polly',
    pokes fun.
'Jolly Mop.' But lies under every full moon,
The spun glass of her body bared and so gleam-still
Her brimming eyes do not tremble or spill
   The dream where the warrior comes, lightning and iron,
    Smashing and burning and rending towards her loin:
      Deep into her pillow her silence pleads.

All day he stares at his furnace
With eyes red-raw, but when she comes they close.
'Polly. Pretty Poll', she cajoles, and rocks him gently.
She caresses, whispers kisses. The blue lids stay shut.
She strikes the cage in a tantrum and swirls out:
 Instantly beak, wings, talons crash
 The bars in conflagration and frenzy,
  And his shriek shakes the house.

The Thought-Fox

I imagine this midnight moment's forest:
Something else is alive
Beside the clock's loneliness
And this blank page where my fingers move.

Through the window I see no star:
Something more near
Though deeper within darkness
Is entering the loneliness:

Cold, delicately as the dark snow,
A fox's nose touches twig, leaf;
Two eyes serve a movement, that now
And again now, and now, and now

Sets neat prints into the snow
Between trees, and warily a lame
Shadow lags by stump and in hollow
Of a body that is bold to come

Across clearings, an eye,
A widening deepening greenness,
Brilliantly, concentratedly,
Coming about its own business

Till, with a sudden sharp hot stink of fox
It enters the dark hole of the head.
The window is starless still; the clock ticks,
The page is printed.

The Horses

I climbed through woods in the hour-before-dawn dark.
Evil air, a frost-making stillness,

Not a leaf, not a bird –
A world cast in frost. I came out above the wood

Where my breath left tortuous statues in the iron light.
But the valleys were draining the darkness

Till the moorline – blackening dregs of the brightening
  grey –
Halved the sky ahead. And I saw the horses:

Huge in the dense grey – ten together –
Megalith-still. They breathed, making no move,

With draped manes and tilted hind-hooves,
Making no sound.

I passed: not one snorted or jerked its head.
Grey silent fragments

Of a grey silent world.

I listened in emptiness on the moor-ridge.
The curlew's tear turned its edge on the silence.

Slowly detail leafed from the darkness. Then the sun
Orange, red, red erupted

Silently, and splitting to its core tore and flung cloud,
Shook the gulf open, showed blue,

And the big planets hanging –
I turned

Stumbling in the fever of a dream, down towards
The dark woods, from the kindling tops,

And came to the horses.
                              There, still they stood,
But now steaming and glistening under the flow of light,

Their draped stone manes, their tilted hind-hooves
Stirring under a thaw while all around them

The frost showed its fires. But still they made no sound.
Not one snorted or stamped,

Their hung heads patient as the horizons,
High over valleys, in the red levelling rays –

In din of the crowded streets, going among the years, the
     faces,
May I still meet my memory in so lonely a place

Between the streams and the red clouds, hearing curlews,
Hearing the horizons endure.

Famous Poet

Stare at the monster: remark
How difficult it is to define just what
Amounts to monstrosity in that
Very ordinary appearance. Neither thin nor fat,
   Hair between light and dark,

   And the general air
Of an apprentice – say, an apprentice house-
Painter amid an assembly of famous
Architects: the demeanour is of mouse,
   Yet is he monster.

   First scrutinize those eyes
For the spark, the effulgence: nothing. Nothing there
But the haggard stony exhaustion of a near-
Finished variety artist. He slumps in his chair
   Like a badly hurt man, half life-size.

   Is it his dreg-boozed inner demon
Still tankarding from tissue and follicle
The vital fire, the spirit electrical
That puts the gloss on a normal hearty male?
   Or is it women?

   The truth – bring it on
With black drapery, drums, and funeral tread
Like a great man's coffin – no, no, he is not dead
But in this truth surely half-buried:
   Once, the humiliation

Of youth and obscurity,
The autoclave of heady ambition trapped,
The fermenting of a yeasty heart stopped –
Burst with such pyrotechnics the dull world gaped
    And 'Repeat that!' still they cry.

    But all his efforts to concoct
The old heroic bang from their money and praise,
From the parent's pointing finger and the child' amaze,
Even from the burning of his wreathed bays,
    Have left him wrecked: wrecked,

    And monstrous, so,
As a Stegosaurus, a lumbering obsolete
Arsenal of gigantic horn and plate
From a time when half the world still burned, set
    To blink behind bars at the zoo.

Song

O lady, when the tipped cup of the moon blessed you
You became soft fire with a cloud's grace;
The difficult stars swam for eyes in your face;
You stood, and your shadow was my place:
You turned, your shadow turned to ice
    O my lady.

O lady, when the sea caressed you
You were a marble of foam, but dumb.
When will the stone open its tomb?
When will the waves give over their foam?
You will not die, nor come home,
    O my lady.

O lady, when the wind kissed you
You made him music for you were a shaped shell.
I follow the waters and the wind still
Since my heart heard it and all to pieces fell
Which your lovers stole, meaning ill,
    O my lady.

O lady, consider when I shall have lost you
The moon's full hands, scattering waste,
The sea's hands, dark from the world's breast,
The world's decay where the wind's hands have passed,
And my head, worn out with love, at rest
In my hands, and my hands full of dust,
    O my lady.

Parlour-Piece

With love so like fire they dared not
Let it out into strawy small talk;
With love so like a flood they dared not
Let out a trickle lest the whole crack,

These two sat speechlessly:
Pale cool tea in tea-cups chaperoned
Stillness, silence, the eyes
Where fire and flood strained.

Secretary

If I should touch her she would shriek and weeping
Crawl off to nurse the terrible wound: all
Day like a starling under the bellies of bulls
She hurries among men, ducking, peeping,

Off in a whirl at the first move of a horn.
At dusk she scuttles down the gauntlet of lust
Like a clockwork mouse. Safe home at last
She mends socks with holes, shirts that are torn,

For father and brother, and a delicate supper cooks:
Goes to bed early, shuts out with the light
Her thirty years, and lies with buttocks tight,
Hiding her lovely eyes until day break.

Soliloquy of a Misanthrope

Whenever I am got under my gravestone,
Sending my flowers up to stare at the church-tower,
Gritting my teeth in the chill from the church-floor,
I shall praise God heartily, to see gone,

As I look round at old acquaintance there,
Complacency from the smirk of every man,
And every attitude showing its bone,
And every mouth confessing its crude shire;

But I shall thank God thrice heartily
To be lying beside women who grimace
Under the commitments of their flesh,
And not out of spite or vanity.

The Dove Breeder

Love struck into his life
Like a hawk into a dovecote.
What a cry went up!
Every gentle pedigree dove
Blindly clattered and beat,
And the mild-mannered dove-breeder
Shrieked at that raider.

He might well wring his hands
And let his tears drop:
He will win no more prizes
With fantails or pouters,
(After all these years
Through third, up through second places
Till they were all world beaters . . .)

Yet he soon dried his tears

Now he rides the morning mist
With a big-eyed hawk on his fist.

Billet-Doux

Here is the magniloquent truth –
His twelve bright brass bands
Diverted down mouseholes –
Walking the town with his head high
And naked as his breath.

I have looked far enough
If now I have found one who does
Not – hold that 'not' to the light – ,
When I walk about in my blood and the air
Beside her, sweeten smiles, peep, cough,

Who sees straight through bogeyman,
The crammed cafés, the ten thousand
Books packed end to end, even my gross bulk,
To the fiery star coming for the eye itself,
And while she can grabs of them what she can.

Love you I do not say I do or might either.
I come to you enforcedly –
Love's a spoiled appetite for some delicacy –
I am driven to your bed and four walls
From bottomlessly breaking night –

If, dispropertied as I am
By the constellations staring me to less
Than what cold, rain and wind neglect,
I do not hold you closer and harder than love
By a desperation, show me no home.

A Modest Proposal

There is no better way to know us
Than as two wolves, come separately to a wood.
Now neither's able to sleep – even at a distance
Distracted by the soft competing pulse
Of the other; nor able to hunt – at every step
Looking backwards and sideways, warying to listen
For the other's slavering rush. Neither can make die
The painful burning of the coal in its heart
Till the other's body and the whole wood is its own.
Then it might sob contentment toward the moon.

Each in a thicket, rage hoarse in its labouring
Chest after a skirmish, licks the rents in its hide,
Eyes brighter than is natural under the leaves
(Where the wren, peeping round a leaf, shrieks out
To see a chink so terrifyingly open
Onto the red smelting of hatred) as each
Pictures a mad final satisfaction.

Suddenly they duck and peer.
                                        And there rides by
The great lord from hunting. His embroidered
Cloak floats, the tail of his horse pours,
And at his stirrup the two great-eyed greyhounds
That day after day bring down the towering stag
Leap like one, making delighted sounds.

Incompatibilities

Desire's a vicious separator in spite
    Of its twisting women round men:
Cold-chisels two selfs single as it welds hot
    Iron of their separates to one.

Old Eden commonplace: something magnets
    And furnaces and with fierce
Hammer-blows the one body on the other knits
    Till the division disappears.

But desire outstrips those hands that a nothing fills,
    It dives into the opposite eyes,
Plummets through blackouts of impassables
    For the star that lights the face,

Each body still straining to follow down
    The maelstrom dark of the other, their limbs flail
Flesh and beat upon
    The inane everywhere of its obstacle,

Each, each second, lonelier and further
    Falling alone through the endless
Without-world of the other, though both here
    Twist so close they choke their cries.

September

We sit late, watching the dark slowly unfold:
No clock counts this.
When kisses are repeated and the arms hold
There is no telling where time is.

It is midsummer: the leaves hang big and still:
Behind the eye a star,
Under the silk of the wrist a sea, tell
Time is nowhere.

We stand; leaves have not timed the summer.
No clock now needs
Tell we have only what we remember:
Minutes uproaring with our heads

Like an unfortunate King's and his Queen's
When the senseless mob rules;
And quietly the trees casting their crowns
Into the pools.

Fallgrief's Girl-Friends

Not that she had no equal, not that she was
His before flesh was his or the world was;
Not that she had the especial excellence
To make her cat-indolence and shrew-mouth
Index to its humanity. Her looks
Were what a good friend would not comment on.
If he made flattery too particular,
Admiring her cookery or lipstick,
Her eyes reflected painfully. Yet not that
He pitied her: he did not pity her.

'Any woman born', he said, 'having
What any woman born cannot but have,
Has as much of the world as is worth more
Than wit or lucky looks can make worth more;
And I, having what I have as a man
Got without choice, and what I have chosen,
City and neighbour and work, am poor enough
To be more than bettered by a worst woman.
Whilst I am this muck of man in this
Muck of existence, I shall not seek more
Than a muck of a woman: wit and lucky looks
Were a ring disabling this pig-snout,
And a tin clasp on this diamond.'

By this he meant to break out of the dream
Where admiration's giddy mannequin
Leads every sense to motley; he meant to stand naked
Awake in the pitch dark where the animal runs,
Where the insects couple as they murder each other,
Where the fish outwait the water.

The chance changed him:
He has found a woman with such wit and looks
He can brag of her in every company.

Two Phases

You had to come
Calling my singularity,
In scorn,
Imprisonment.

It contained content
That, now, at liberty
In your generous embrace,
As once, in rich Rome,
Caractacus,
I mourn.

When the labour was for love
He did but touch at the tool
And holiday ran prodigal.

Now, stripped to the skin,
Can scarcely keep alive,
Sweats his stint out,
No better than a blind mole
That burrows for its lot
Of the flaming moon and sun
Down some black hole.

The Decay of Vanity

Now it is seven years since you were the Queen
That crowned me King; and six years since your ghost
Left your body cold in my arms as a stone.

Then for three years I did heart-brokenly
Embalm your remains; but after that
I let your eye shrink and your body dry,

And had forgotten whether you still hung here,
Or had gone, with all the old junk, out onto the heap
Where scraggy cockerels rake and stab and peer –

Till this man loomed up with your shrunken head.
He, I see, by the majesty in his stride,
Dreams he sweeps some great queen towards his bed,

Yet skulks by me, swagger as he dare:
This royal trophy, which, in a world of pride,
Makes him your King, makes him my scavenger.

Fair Choice

Fair choice? The appearance of the devil! Suave
Complicity with your vacillation
To your entire undoing! A midwife
Delivering darlings to your indecision –
Twins, quick in their cradle, loud as alive,

But rivalling eithers! Before choice's fairness
Humanized both, barbarously you might
Have made beast-death of the one a sacrifice
To the god-head of the other, and buried its right
Before it opened eyes to be emulous.

But now that your twins wail, are wide-eyed –
(Tugging between them some frivolous heirloom)
You must cold murder the one and force-feed
With your remorse the other and protect him from
The vengeful voluble ghost of the twin dead.

Or you must bend your dilemma-feebled spine
Under – as if nobly and under tons –
Rearing both fairly. The spilt blood be your own!
Your every glance shall see one of your twins
An Abel to the other's bloody Cain.

The Conversion of the Reverend Skinner

'Dare you reach so high, girl, from the gutter of the street?'
She slapped his cheek and turned his tongue right over:
'Your church has cursed me till I am black as it:
The devil has my preference forever.'
She spoke. An upstart gentleman
Flashed his golden palm to her and she ran.

But he lay there stretched full length in the gutter.
He swore to live on dog-licks for ten years.
'My pride has been the rotten heart of the matter.'
His eyes dwelt with the quick ankles of whores.
To mortify pride he hailed each one:
'This is the ditch to pitch abortions in.'

He stared up at the dark and he cursed that;
'As if my own heart were not bad enough,
But heaven itself must blacken with the rot!'
Then he saw the thin moon staggering through the rough
Wiping her wound. And he rose wild
And sought and blest only what was defiled.

Complaint

Aged Mother, Mary, even though – when that thing
Leaped hedge in the dark lane (or grabbed your heel
On the attic stair) by smell of man and coarse
Canvas he wore was disguised too well-ill
A scorching and dizzying blue apparition; –

Though that Jack Horner's hedge-scratched pig-splitting arm,
Grubbing his get among your lilies, was a comet
That plunged through the flowery whorl to your
   womb-root,
And grew a man's face on its burning head; –

Though no prompt thundercrack, no knave's remorse
Kneeling in the arch of lightning, fisting his guilt,
But the times quiet with God's satisfaction; –

Though you swallowed the honey of a parable,
No forced fistful of meat-and-potato fact –

History's grown gross-bellied, not bright-eyed.

Phaetons

Angrier, angrier, suddenly the near-madman
In mid-vehemence rolls back his eye
And lurches to his feet –

Under each sense the other four hurtle and thunder
Under the skull's front the horses of the sun

The gentle reader in his silent room
Loses the words in mid-sentence –

The world has burned away beneath his book
A tossing upside-down team drags him on fire
Among the monsters of the zodiac.

Egg-Head

A leaf's otherness,
The whaled monstered sea-bottom, eagled peaks
And stars that hang over hurtling endlessness,
    With manslaughtering shocks

    Are let in on his sense:
So many a one has dared to be struck dead
Peeping through his fingers at the world's ends,
    Or at an ant's head.

    But better defence
Than any militant pride are the freebooting crass
Veterans of survival and those champions
    Forgetfulness, madness.

    Brain in deft opacities,
Walled in translucencies, shuts out the world's knocking
With a welcome, and to wide-eyed deafnesses
    Of prudence lets it speak.

    Long the eggshell head's
Fragility rounds and resists receiving the flash
Of the sun, the bolt of the earth: and feeds
    On the yolk's dark and hush

    Of a helplessness coming
By feats of torpor, by circumventing sleights
Of stupefaction, juggleries of benumbing,
    By lucid sophistries of sight

To a staturing 'I am',
To the upthrust affirmative head of a man.
Braggart-browed complacency in most calm
  Collusion with his own

  Dewdrop frailty
Must stop the looming mouth of the earth with a pin-
Point cipher, with a blank-stare courtesy
  Confront it and preen,

  Spurn it muck under
His foot-clutch, and, opposing his eye's flea-red
Fly-catching fervency to the whelm of the sun,
  Trumpet his own ear dead.

The Man Seeking Experience Enquires
His Way of a Drop of Water

'This water droplet, charity of the air,
Out of the watched blue immensity –
(Where, where are the angels?) out of the draught in the
   door,
The Tuscarora, the cloud, the cup of tea,
The sweating victor and the decaying dead bird –
This droplet has travelled far and studied hard.

'Now clings on the cream paint of our kitchen wall.
Aged eye! This without heart-head-nerve lens
Which saw the first and earth-centering jewel
Spark upon darkness, behemoth bulk and lumber
Out of the instant flash, and man's hand
Hoist him upright, still hangs clear and round.

'Having studied a journey in the high
Cathedralled brain, the mole's ear, the fish's ice,
The abattoir of the tiger's artery,
The slum of the dog's bowel, and there is no place
His bright look has not bettered, and problem none
But he has brought it to solution.

'Venerable elder! Let us learn of you.
Read us a lesson, a plain lesson how
Experience has worn or made you anew,
That on this humble kitchen wall hang now,
O dew that condensed of the breath of the Word
On the mirror of the syllable of the Word.'

So he spoke, aloud, grandly, then stood
For an answer, knowing his own nature all
Droplet-kin, sisters and brothers of lymph and blood,
Listened for himself to speak for the drop's self.
This droplet was clear simple water still.
It no more responded than the hour-old child

Does to finger-toy or coy baby-talk,
But who lies long, long and frowningly
Unconscious under the shock of its own quick
After that first alone-in-creation cry
When into the mesh of sense, out of the dark,
Blundered the world-shouldering monstrous 'I'.

Meeting

He smiles in a mirror, shrinking the whole
Sun-swung zodiac of light to a trinket shape
   On the rise of his eye: it is a role

In which he can fling a cape,
And outloom life like Faustus. But once when
   On an empty mountain slope

A black goat clattered and ran
Towards him, and set forefeet firm on a rock
   Above and looked down

A square-pupilled yellow-eyed look,
The black devil head against the blue air,
   What gigantic fingers took

Him up and on a bare
Palm turned him close under an eye
   That was like a living hanging hemisphere

And watched his blood's gleam with a ray
Slow and cold and ferocious as a star
   Till the goat clattered away.

Wind

This house has been far out at sea all night,
The woods crashing through darkness, the booming hills,
Winds stampeding the fields under the window
Floundering black astride and blinding wet

Till day rose; then under an orange sky
The hills had new places, and wind wielded
Blade-light, luminous black and emerald,
Flexing like the lens of a mad eye.

At noon I scaled along the house-side as far as
The coal-house door. I dared once to look up –
Through the brunt wind that dented the balls of my eyes
The tent of the hills drummed and strained its guyrope,

The fields quivering, the skyline a grimace,
At any second to bang and vanish with a flap:
The wind flung a magpie away and a black-
Back gull bent like an iron bar slowly. The house

Rang like some fine green goblet in the note
That any second would shatter it. Now deep
In chairs, in front of the great fire, we grip
Our hearts and cannot entertain book, thought,

Or each other. We watch the fire blazing,
And feel the roots of the house move, but sit on,
Seeing the window tremble to come in,
Hearing the stones cry out under the horizons.

October Dawn

October is marigold, and yet
A glass half full of wine left out

To the dark heaven all night, by dawn
Has dreamed a premonition

Of ice across its eye as if
The ice-age had begun its heave.

The lawn overtrodden and strewn
From the night before, and the whistling green

Shrubbery are doomed. Ice
Has got its spearhead into place.

First a skin, delicately here
Restraining a ripple from the air;

Soon plate and rivet on pond and brook;
Then tons of chain and massive lock

To hold rivers. Then, sound by sight
Will Mammoth and Sabre-tooth celebrate

Reunion while a fist of cold
Squeezes the fire at the core of the world,

Squeezes the fire at the core of the heart,
And now it is about to start.

Roarers in a Ring

Snow fell as for Wenceslas.
   The moor foamed like a white
Running sea. A starved fox
   Stared at the inn light.

In the red gridded glare of peat,
   Faces sweating like hams,
Farmers roared their Christmas Eve
   Out of the low beams.

Good company kept a laugh in the air
   As if they tossed a ball
To top the skip of a devil that
   Struck at it with his tail,

Or struck at the man who held it long.
   They so tossed laughter up
You would have thought that if they did not
   Laugh, they must weep.

Therefore the ale went round and round.
   Their mouths flung wide
The cataract of a laugh, lest
   Silence drink blood.

And their eyes were screwed so tight,
   While their grand bellies shook –
O their flesh would drop to dust
   At the first sober look.

The air was new as a razor,
 The moor looked like the moon,
When they all went roaring homewards
 An hour before dawn.

Those living images of their deaths
 Better than with skill
Blindly and rowdily balanced
 Gently took their fall

While the world under their footsoles
 Went whirling still
Gay and forever, in the bottomless black
 Silence through which it fell.

Vampire

You hosts are almost glad he gate-crashed: see,
How his eyes brighten on the whisky, how his wit
Tumbles the company like a lightning stroke, –
You marvel where he gets his energy from . . .

But that same instant, here, far underground,
This fusty carcass stirs its shroud and swells.

'Stop, stop, oh for God's sake, stop!' you shriek
As your tears run down, but he goes on and on
Mercilessly till you think your ribs must crack . . .

While this carcass's eyes grimace, stitched
In the cramp of an ordeal, and a squeeze of blood
Crawls like scorpions into its hair.

You plead, limp, dangling in his mad voice, till
With a sudden blood-spittling cough, he chokes: he leaves
Trembling, soon after. You slump back down in a chair
Cold as a leaf, your heart scarcely moving . . .

Deep under the city's deepest stone
This grinning sack is bursting with your blood.

Childbirth

When, on the bearing mother, death's
Door opened its furious inch,
Instant of struggling and blood,
The commonplace became so strange

There was not looking at table or chair:
Miracle struck out the brain
Of order and ordinary: bare
Onto the heart the earth dropped then

With whirling quarters, the axle cracked,
Through that miracle-breached bed
All the dead could have got back;
With shriek and heave and spout of blood

The huge-eyed looming horde from
Under the floor of the heart, that run
To the madman's eye-corner came
Deafening towards light, whereon

A child whimpered upon the bed,
Frowning ten-toed ten-fingered birth
Put the skull back about the head
Righted the stagger of the earth.

The Hag

The old story went that the cajoling hag
Fattened the pretty princess within a fence
Of barbs the spiders poked their eight eyes out in
Even, the points were so close, fattened her
With pastry pies and would not let her incline
One inch toward the threshold from the table
Lest she slip off the hag's dish and exchange
The hag's narrow intestine for the wide world.
And this hag had to lie in a certain way
At night lest the horrible angular black hatred
Poke through her side and surprise the pretty princess
Who was well-deceived by this posture of love.

Now here is an old hag, as I see,
Has got this story direly drastically wrong,
Who has dragged her pretty daughter home from college,
Who has locked up her pretty eyes in a brick house
And has sworn her pretty mouth shall rot like fruit
Before the world shall make a jam of it
To spread on every palate. And so saying,
She must lie perforce at night in a certain way
Lest the heart break through her side and burst the walls
And surprise her daughter with an extravagance
Of tearful love, who finds it easier
To resign her hope of a world wide with love,
And even to rot in the dark, but easier under
Nine bolts of spite than on one leash of love.

Law in the Country of the Cats

When two men meet for the first time in all
Eternity and outright hate each other,
Not as a beggar-man and a rich man,
Not as cuckold-maker and cuckold,
Not as bully and delicate boy, but
As dog and wolf because their blood before
They are aware has bristled into their hackles,
Because one has clubbed the other to death
With the bottle first broached to toast their transaction
And swears to God he went helpless black-out
While they were mixing smiles, facts have sacked
The oath of the pious witness who judged all men
As a one humble brotherhood of man.

When two men at first meeting hate each other
Even in passing, without words, in the street,
They are not likely to halt as if remembering
They once met somewhere, where in fact they met,
And discuss 'universal brotherhood',
'Love of humanity and each fellow-man',
Or 'the growing likelihood of perpetual peace',
But if, by chance, they do meet, so mistaking,
There will be that moment's horrible pause
As each looks into the gulf in the eye of the other,
Then a flash of violent incredible action,
Then one man letting his brains gently to the gutter,
And one man bursting into the police station
Crying: 'Let Justice be done. I did it, I.'

Invitation to the Dance

The condemned prisoner stirred, but could not stir:
Cold had shackled the blood-prints of the knout.
The light of his death's dawn put the dark out.
He lay, his lips numb to the frozen floor.
He dreamed some other prisoner was dragged out –
Nightmare of command in the dawn, and a shot.
The bestial gaoler's boot was at his ear.

Upon his sinews torturers had grown strong,
The inquisitor old against a tongue that could not,
Being torn out, plead even for death.
All bones were shattered, the whole body unstrung.
Horses, plunging apart towards North and South,
Tore his heart up by the shrieking root.
He was flung to the blow-fly and the dog's fang.

Pitched onto his mouth in a black ditch
All spring he heard the lovers rustle and sigh.
The sun stank. Rats worked at him secretly.
Rot and maggot stripped him stitch by stitch.
Yet still this dream engaged his vanity:
That could he get upright he would dance and cry
Shame on every shy or idle wretch.

The Casualty

Farmers in the fields, housewives behind steamed windows,
Watch the burning aircraft across the blue sky float,
As if a firefly and a spider fought,
Far above the trees, between the washing hung out.
They wait with interest for the evening news.

But already, in a brambled ditch, suddenly-smashed
Stems twitch. In the stubble a pheasant
Is craning every way in astonishment.
The hare that hops up, quizzical, hesitant,
Flattens ears and tears madly away and the wren warns.

Some, who saw fall, smoke beckons. They jostle above,
They peer down a sunbeam as if they expected there
A snake in the gloom of the brambles or a rare flower, –
See the grave of dead leaves heave suddenly, hear
It was a man fell out of the air alive,

Hear now his groans and senses groping. They rip
The slum of weeds, leaves, barbed coils; they raise
A body that as the breeze touches it glows,
Branding their hands on his bones. Now that he has
No spine, against heaped sheaves they prop him up,

Arrange his limbs in order, open his eye,
Then stand, helpless as ghosts. In a scene
Melting in the August noon, the burned man
Bulks closer greater flesh and blood than their own,
As suddenly the heart's beat shakes his body and the eye

Widens childishly. Sympathies
Fasten to the blood like flies. Here's no heart's more
Open or large than a fist clenched, and in there
Holding close complacency its most dear
Unscratchable diamond. The tears of their eyes

Too tender to let break, start to the edge
Of such horror close as mourners can,
Greedy to share all that is undergone,
Grimace, gasp, gesture of death. Till they look down
On the handkerchief at which his eye stares up.

Bayonet Charge

Suddenly he awoke and was running – raw
In raw-seamed hot khaki, his sweat heavy,
Stumbling across a field of clods towards a green hedge
That dazzled with rifle fire, hearing
Bullets smacking the belly out of the air –
He lugged a rifle numb as a smashed arm;
The patriotic tear that had brimmed in his eye
Sweating like molten iron from the centre of his chest, –

In bewilderment then he almost stopped –
In what cold clockwork of the stars and the nations
Was he the hand pointing that second? He was running
Like a man who has jumped up in the dark and runs
Listening between his footfalls for the reason
Of his still running, and his foot hung like
Statuary in mid-stride. Then the shot-slashed furrows

Threw up a yellow hare that rolled like a flame
And crawled in a threshing circle, its mouth wide
Open silent, its eyes standing out.
He plunged past with his bayonet toward the green hedge.
King, honour, human dignity, etcetera
Dropped like luxuries in a yelling alarm
To get out of that blue crackling air
His terror's touchy dynamite.

Griefs for Dead Soldiers

I

Mightiest, like some universal cataclysm,
Will be the unveiling of their cenotaph:
The crowds will stand struck, like the painting of a terror
Where the approaching planet, a half-day off,
Hangs huge above the thin skulls of the silenced birds;
Each move, each sound, a fresh-cut epitaph –
Monstrousness of the moment making the air stone.

Though thinly, the bugle will then cry,
The dead drum tap, and the feet of the columns
And the sergeant-major's voice blown about by the wind
Make these dead magnificent, their souls
Scrolled and supporting the sky, and the national sorrow,
Over the crowds that know of no other wound,
Permanent stupendous victory.

II

Secretest, tiniest, there, where the widow watches on the table
The telegram opening of its own accord
Inescapably and more terribly than any bomb
That dives to the cellar and lifts the house. The bared
Words shear the hawsers of love that now lash
Back in darkness, blinding and severing. To a world
Lonely as her skull and little as her heart

The doors and windows open like great gates to a hell.
Still she will carry cups from table to sink.
She cannot build her sorrow into a monument
And walk away from it. Closer than thinking
The dead man hangs around her neck, but never
Close enough to be touched, or thanked even,
For being all that remains in a world smashed.

III

Truest, and only just, here, where since
The battle passed the grass has sprung up
Surprisingly in the valleyful of dead men.
Under the blue sky heavy crow and black fly move.
Flowers bloom prettily to the edge of the mass grave
Where spades hack, and the diggers grunt and sweat.
Among the flowers the dead wait like brides

To surrender their limbs; thud of another body flung
Down, the jolted shape of a face, earth into the mouth –
Moment that could annihilate a watcher!
Cursing the sun that makes their work long
Or the black lively flies that bite their wrists,
The burial party works with a craftsman calm.
Weighing their grief by the ounce, and burying it.

Six Young Men

The celluloid of a photograph holds them well, –
Six young men, familiar to their friends.
Four decades that have faded and ochre-tinged
This photograph have not wrinkled the faces or the hands.
Though their cocked hats are not now fashionable,
Their shoes shine. One imparts an intimate smile,
One chews a grass, one lowers his eyes, bashful,
One is ridiculous with cocky pride –
Six months after this picture they were all dead.

All are trimmed for a Sunday jaunt. I know
That bilberried bank, that thick tree, that black wall,
Which are there yet and not changed. From where these sit
You hear the water of seven streams fall
To the roarer in the bottom, and through all
The leafy valley a rumouring of air go.
Pictured here, their expressions listen yet,
And still that valley has not changed its sound
Though their faces are four decades under the ground.

This one was shot in an attack and lay
Calling in the wire, then this one, his best friend,
Went out to bring him in and was shot too;
And this one, the very moment he was warned
From potting at tin-cans in no-man's land,
Fell back dead with his rifle-sights shot away.
The rest, nobody knows what they came to,
But come to the worst they must have done, and held it
Closer than their hope; all were killed.

Here see a man's photograph,
The locket of a smile, turned overnight
Into the hospital of his mangled last
Agony and hours; see bundled in it
His mightier-than-a-man dead bulk and weight:
And on this one place which keeps him alive
(In his Sunday best) see fall war's worst
Thinkable flash and rending, onto his smile
Forty years rotting into soil.

That man's not more alive whom you confront
And shake by the hand, see hale, hear speak loud,
Than any of these six celluloid smiles are,
Nor prehistoric or fabulous beast more dead;
No thought so vivid as their smoking blood:
To regard this photograph might well dement,
Such contradictory permanent horrors here
Smile from the single exposure and shoulder out
One's own body from its instant and heat.

Two Wise Generals

'Not as Black Douglas, bannered, trumpeted,
Who hacked for the casked heart flung to the enemy,
Letting the whole air flow breakneck with blood
Till he fell astride that handful, you and I

Come, two timid and ageing generals
To parley, and to divide the territory
Upon a map, and get honour, and by
This satisfaction part with regiments whole.'

They entered the lit tent, in no hurry to grab.
Apart in darkness twinkled their armies
Like two safe towns. Thus they drank, joked, waxed wise –
So heavily medalled never need fear stab.

The treaty sealed, lands allotted (and a good third
Stuffed down their tunic fronts' private estate)
They left the empty bottle. The tent-lamp out,
They lurched away in the knee-high mist, hearing the first
   bird,

Towards separate camps.
                              Now, one a late dew-moth
Eyes, as he sways, among the still tents. The other roars
   'Guard!'
As a fox ducks from the silent parapet. Both
Have found their sleeping armies massacred.

The Ancient Heroes and the
Bomber Pilot

With nothing to brag about but the size of their hearts,
Tearing boar-flesh and swilling ale,
A fermenting of huge-chested braggarts

Got nowhere by sitting still
To hear some timorous poet enlarge heroisms,
To suffer their veins stifle and swell –

Soon, far easier, imagination all flames,
In the white orbit of a sword,
Their chariot-wheels tumbling the necks of screams,

In a glory of hair and beard,
They thinned down their fat fulsome blood in war,
Replenishing both bed and board,

Making their own good news, restuffing their dear
Fame with fresh sacks-full of heads,
Roaring, burdened, back over the wet moor.

When archaeologists dig their remainder out –
Bits of bone, rust, –
The grandeur of their wars humbles my thought.

Even though I can boast
The enemy capital will jump to a fume
At a turn of my wrist

And the huge earth be shaken in its frame, –
I am pale.
When I imagine one of those warriors in the room

And hear his heart-beat burl
The centuries are a stopped clock; my heart
Is cold and small.

The Martyrdom of Bishop Farrar

Burned by Bloody Mary's men at Caermarthen. 'If I
flinch from the pain of the burning, believe not the doctrine
that I have preached.' (His words on being chained to the
stake.)

Bloody Mary's venomous flames can curl;
They can shrivel sinew and char bone
Of foot, ankle, knee, and thigh, and boil
Bowels, and drop his heart a cinder down;
And her soldiers can cry, as they hurl
Logs in the red rush: 'This is her sermon.'

The sullen-jowled watching Welsh townspeople
Hear him crack in the fire's mouth; they see what
Black oozing twist of stuff bubbles the smell
That tars and retches their lungs: no pulpit
Of his ever held their eyes so still,
Never, as now his agony, his wit.

An ignorant means to establish ownership
Of his flock! Thus their shepherd she seized
And knotted him into this blazing shape
In their eyes, as if such could have cauterized
The trust they turned towards him, and branded on
Its stump her claim, to outlaw question.

So it might have been: seeing their exemplar
And teacher burned for his lessons to black bits,
Their silence might have disowned him to her,
And hung up what he had taught with their Welsh hats:
Who sees his blasphemous father struck by fire
From heaven, might well be heard to speak no oaths.

But the fire that struck here, come from Hell even,
Kindled little heavens in his words
As he fed his body to the flame alive.
Words which, before they will be dumbly spared,
Will burn their body and be tongued with fire
Make paltry folly of flesh and this world's air.

When they saw what annuities of hours
And comfortable blood he burned to get
His words a bare honouring in their ears,
The shrewd townsfolk pocketed them hot:
Stamp was not current but they rang and shone
As good gold as any queen's crown.

Gave all he had, and yet the bargain struck
To a merest farthing his whole agony,
His body's cold-kept miserdom of shrieks
He gave uncounted, while out of his eyes,
Out of his mouth, fire like a glory broke,
And smoke burned his sermons into the skies.